My Life, My Dance, My Soul

This book was made possible with support and funding from the National Arts Council.

National Arts Council
an Agency of the Department of Sport, Arts & Culture

First published by Jacana Media (Pty) Ltd in 2023

10 Orange Street
Sunnyside
Auckland Park 2092
South Africa
+2711 628 3200
www.jacana.co.za

© Gregory Maqoma, 2023
Cover photograph © Gregory Maqoma
   (photo by Arthur Dlamini)

All rights reserved.

ISBN 978-1-4314-3382-7

Cover design by Toby Newsome
Editing by Henrietta Rose-Innes
Proofreading by Lara Jacob
Set in Merriweather 10/15PT
Printed by ABC Press, Cape Town
Job no. 004084

See a complete list of Jacana titles at
www.jacana.co.za

My Life, My Dance, My Soul

The Story of Gregory Maqoma

Gregory Maqoma
with Lorato Trok

*To my father, Peter Lizo Maqoma, as well as
to a dear friend and brother, Pule Kgaratsi*

Contents

	Introduction	1
1	What's in a name?	7
2	Fathers and sons	13
3	Born into royalty	23
4	Growing up in Soweto	29
5	Finding my spirit	37
6	A brotherhood of trust	43
7	Moving into dance	53
8	An African odyssey	59
9	Losing a father – and finding forefathers	67
10	Exit/Exist	75
11	Becoming me	83
12	Choreography: A passion like no other	91
	Appendix 1: Theatre productions	101
	Appendix 2: Awards and accolades	111
	A note from Lorato Trok	115
	Bibliography	119
	About the authors	123

Photo by Arthur Dlamini

Introduction

A journalist once asked me, 'What does art mean to you?' I paused for a while, looking for an intelligent answer. It was not forthcoming ... and then a small voice whispered in me: 'Life – art is life.' I realised the truth of it: when I look back at my life, everything I've done has been a form of art and in service to art.

I was born and raised in Orlando East, Soweto, the oldest township in Johannesburg. Growing up there taught me about the complexities and challenges of the world. I come from a place ravaged by conflict, greed, intolerance, corruption; but am also blessed by the beauty of its people – deeply rooted in tradition and culture, connected to the landscape. It is a place full of possibility and contradiction.

As a boy, I was always the entertainer in my community, dancing and singing along to the pop hits of the day. Of course, this was all a huge embarrassment to my father, who wanted me to be a soccer player or a doctor. But the seed of an artist's life had been planted. I did not know that it would grow to take me around the world – six continents, over 100 cities – and that it would be filled with so much joy and pain.

More than ever, in these challenging times, we need the arts, and artists, to remind us that we are all human, each with a role to play. My art, my dance, has opened up so many possibilities and opportunities for me. Travelling, thus creating amazing connections and friendships, has given me the power to engage with those who can change the world we live in for the better.

In this memoir I hope to celebrate and acknowledge those who have touched my life, and those whom I have touched in return. I dedicate this book to my father, Peter Lizo Maqoma, and to my dear friend and brother, Pule Kgaratsi. Both men were fathers to me, in different ways; their passing left me broken.

I have so many other people to thank and honour that it is impossible to mention everyone. Firstly, Sylvia Glasser, who nurtured me in my early dance years and has continued to be a constant supporter. I have to mention Claire Verlet, dance programmer and producer at Paris Théâtre de la Ville. She first invited me to France in 2001 when she was working at Centre National de la Dance in Pantin, Paris; our connection continued through my pieces *Beauty Trilogy*, *Southern Bound Comfort* and *Exit/Exist*. I am hugely indebted to her – it is no accident that France has hosted more performances of my work than any other country, including my own.

Without the dedication of my team at Vuyani Dance Theatre, the dance company I created in 1999, none of this would have been possible. 'Vuyani' means joy, and my theatre is a platform where joy can rise above pain, where humanity can manifest beyond egos, and legacies can be built. As artists, as we write our scripts and imagine our dances, as we travel to other worlds, we think also about our legacy and our role in society. We think about our central character, the one who leads the dance; but most importantly, we think of how we want the story to end – what we want to leave behind for future generations.

My goal is to inspire a new generation of dance makers and performers. When I look at the dancers I work with, young children in our communities, I am amazed by their creative minds, how their bodies respond to dance and how this can bring healing. By the time a project is wrapped up, I go home knowing that dancers are among the most powerful beings I know; they are able to tap into their own emotions, and ignite purpose and hope in others. And I feel reassured that more than enough genius, pride, energy and imagination exists in the world to fulfil the promise of art: to heal our broken souls, gives us purpose and restore hope that has been lost.

Gregory Vuyani Maqoma, 2023

Photo by Marijke Willemse

Gregory holding his mother's birthday cake, age 7

— 1 —
What's in a name?

My mother's family, the Mofokengs, were descended from the proud Basotho Ba Pudungwana clan of the Bafokeng in Lesotho. In the 1940s they settled in Orlando East, where I grew up. My father's family came from the Beaufort West area in the Eastern Cape, descended from the royal Amarharhabe division of the Xhosa nation. His parents moved to Orlando East to look for better job prospects in the big city.

My father Lizo was born in 1953, the second son in a family of five children. My mother Agnes was born in the same year. Their love story began in the 1970s, when the teenagers lived across the street from each other in Soweto. I came along on 16 October 1973 – an unexpected surprise for the young couple. They were only 23 and with a three-year-old son to feed, when the uprisings of 1976 engulfed Soweto.

At first I lived with my mother Agnes and maternal grandmother Mampati Francinah Mofokeng in Orlando East. My mother named me Thabang Mofokeng – in the Basotho tradition, a child born out of wedlock is claimed by the mother's family and given their name. I grew up speaking Sesotho. My mother says I was a happy child, though as a toddler I was known to throw tantrums and not speak to anyone for hours, no matter how much my family tried to trick me into talking.

I was sent to Sesotho Ditawana Primary School in Orlando East. 'Ditawana' means 'young lions', and indeed, the school helped us face the world like hungry lions. Our parents were busy working, surviving the harsh realities of life under apartheid; it left them little time to attend to their growing 'lions'. The teachers at school were our guardians, trying to give us an education that would grant us opportunities our parents never had. I can't blame them for any shortcomings as the curriculum was dictated by the government; this was at the height of Bantu Education, designed to teach African children to serve the privileged.

Because my parents' homes were just a street apart, I hopped between houses, happy to soak up both Sotho and Xhosa cultures. Neither was elevated above the other. This dual identity made me who I was – it was the full expression of my humanity. But when my parents married in 1978, my mother and I moved into my father's house. And everything changed.

My father was a traditionalist and very conservative. He wasted no time in changing my name to Gregory Vuyani Maqoma – the first name English, because he believed it would benefit me when I was old enough to work. I hated it. He also declared that no language but isiXhosa be spoken in his house. This became a source of huge friction: I would rebel by speaking Sesotho with my mother and maternal grandmother, only switching to isiXhosa with my father's family.

He did not like the way I spoke isiXhosa and he did not make the transition easy for me. In Sesotho, the letter *r* has a soft intonation, almost like a purr. My father demanded that I learn how to pronounce my new name with no Sesotho accent. There was no explanation, no discussion. Instead, he'd lock me in my bedroom for hours, forcing me to write the letter *r* over and over and pronounce it hundreds of times, shouting from the other room for me to repeat it until my throat hurt. Some days he'd leave the house in disgust, and I'd carry on chanting the letter without realising there was no one home. For many years, I blocked this painful memory.

Because of all this, the name 'Gregory' became a burden to me. I did like my isiXhosa name, Vuyani. 'Thabang Vuyani Maqoma' would have worked just fine – both names mean 'happiness'. But no, I was stuck with the English 'Gregory', with its hard and unforgiving *r*.

To make matters worse, my father insisted that I be baptised at the Maqoma family church, St John's Anglican Church, even though I'd already been rightfully baptised at my mother's Dutch Reformed Church as a baby. My aunt was a congregant at Grace Bible Church in Soweto, and she'd made sure I was baptised in her church too! So, three times baptised, three churches to serve.

Years later, applying for my identity document, I was defeated once again when the ID book came back saying only 'Gregory Maqoma'. It felt like the Maqoma ancestors were conspiring against me. I had no choice but to continue to exist as Gregory.

All these years later, I've long made peace with my name. But I confess to still feeling a small lump in my throat when I'm addressed as 'Gregory'. To my family, I remained Vuyani. And when I later came to name my dance company, I proudly gave it the name I was denied by the government: Vuyani Dance Theatre.

Gregory with his dad, lighting candles on his mother's birthday cake, age 7

— 2 —
Fathers and sons

My father was an extremely upright and conscientious person: a man of his word, a strict traditionalist and an even stricter father. His attention to detail was remarkable, at home and at work. He'd completed his high school education before the 1976 Soweto uprisings that challenged Afrikaans as a language of learning and teaching in township schools, and landed a job as a clerk at a government clinic in Orlando East because of his excellent grasp of Afrikaans. For my father, schooling was a priority.

He always impressed upon me my

position as his first-born son: the one who would carry the family name and take the reins from his father and forefathers. I was to inherit all of that responsibility – and all those expectations.

I found it difficult to come to terms with my father's harsh discipline. I was also confined to home: the political violence of the times meant we were often not able to play outside. As a result, I was a lonely and unhappy child.

One outlet was the Boy Scouts. I joined in primary school, and every Wednesday donned their khaki shirt and shorts. The values of cleanliness, resilience and self-discipline was instilled in us, and we were taught to survive in nature, outside of our comfort zones. Crucially, several scouting activities involved dancing and acting. This was where I learned so many of the skills that I still put into my work today: routine, discipline, formation, precision, rhythm.

My mother and I were very close. She understood I was different and helped me to communicate and express myself. She told me I was beautiful, and that I should smile more. My relationship with her mattered to me more than anything, and the bond we forged was unbreakable.

As a boy, I became the entertainer in my community. I'd steal my mother's wigs and transform myself into one of my favourites – Michael Jackson or Tina Turner. I knew how to channel their performances: every lyric, every move. With each costume change, a seed was planted for my later vocation. These performances were also a way of escaping the debilitating social and political turmoil of 1980s Soweto.

My father and I fought over everything, but especially my mother's attention. I believe he was resentful of our relationship, and despised the way she adored me. Often I felt he only stayed with her because he wanted to take her eyes away from me. I resented my father for his control and possessiveness, and became increasingly protective of my mother. Although he never became physical with us, he ran his household with an iron fist, and she did not escape his strictness.

But he loved me in his own way. He was a soccer fan and insisted that I play; he'd pick me up and put me on his shoulders and take me to matches at Orlando Stadium. I don't think he ever realised how little interest I had in the game. When I was about nine, we lost a school soccer match because of me. When the ball appeared in the sky above me, I froze – and caught the ball in my arms! Of course, the opposition got a penalty. I could hear my father screaming at me from the sidelines. I ran home, too ashamed to watch the end of the game. My dad, perhaps even more embarrassed, made me wash the entire team's white socks as punishment.

My family were devout Christians, particularly on my father's side, and at times this brought them into conflict with tradition. For example, when my younger brother Langa was born when I was 12, he was originally named Wengu, after our grandfather. But when he was two, he started to fall ill. No doctor could find the cause of his frequent sickness. Only when my mother consulted a traditional healer did the reason become clear: it had been a mistake to name him after my grandfather, as it was deemed a form of disrespect and against custom to say his name out loud.

In the end, my parents had to slaughter a goat to ask for the ancestors' forgiveness and rename the little boy. They decided on Langa, which means 'The one that brings the light'.

I always knew that Langa was different – that he possessed something unique. From a young age he loved animals; he was always chasing locusts, which he'd keep in a glass jar with air-holes in the lid. He soon became known for this in the neighbourhood, and our home was transformed into a mini zoo. Tensions brewed between him and my parents over cleaning up after his 'livestock', and he didn't approve of the dog being in the yard, who would disturb his beloved chickens, doves and locusts!

Langa showed signs of being gifted with certain powers from very early on. When he was 14, he disappeared for a few days from home. After a panicked search, he returned, saying that he'd been in the mountains, a secluded place south-east of Johannesburg. He described meeting 'Umkhulu' (grandfather), a man on a horse wearing a Basotho blanket. This sounded very much like our maternal grandfather, who had been a traditional healer and had passed on before any of us children were born. This encounter was clearly a sign that the gifts of healing had been passed on to Langa.

My father wasn't having any of it – he called it demonic. But Langa continued to display his gift, sometimes walking into random people's homes, climbing onto their roofs to remove spells that were making them sick. We'd only find out about this when family members came to our house with gifts to thank Langa for his help. Langa was also being pressured by Umkhulu to start his Ukuthwasa journey (the 'calling' to learn more about traditional medicine and healing). It was only years later, after my father's passing, that Langa finally accepted his gift as a traditional healer. After he passed grade 12, he was initiated by other traditional healers.

My youngest brother, Mncedisi, arrived when I was 19. He and my father were very close. He loved football and was incredibly gifted at it; soccer coaches would line up at our gate, asking for him to play for their teams. It was a beautiful thing to see, this growing father-child relationship; I had missed out on that. As Mncedisi was so much younger than me, I also played a fatherly role.

In the beginning I struggled to bond with my siblings: I was so much older when they were born, and my father never really made me feel like I belonged to the family. By the time my brothers were grown ups, I'd long moved out of the family home. But our relationship changed over time. My mother always put family first and put effort into ensuring that we boys got along well. As adults, we three have remained close and celebrate holidays together.

Things eventually got so bad between me and my father that my paternal grandmother intervened. When I was 15, she decided that I should go and live with my aunt, Yalezwa Makana, in Pimville. Even though I felt like I was being shipped away like goods, the thought of not living under my father's thumb was exciting.

My aunt's marriage had ended and she'd moved from the Eastern Cape, where she'd worked as an administrator. At first she'd stayed in our tiny two-room house, but had eventually managed to buy a house in Pimville in a new development called Baxter. I became a big brother to her three children; we remain very close.

Meanwhile, my mother was lavishing affection on a dog. She'd always wanted a daughter, so when she got a female dog, she was happy to raise it like an adopted child. The dog followed her around, growing increasingly jealous of anyone touching her, especially me. As tiny as the dog was, she had a fearsome bite. Still, I grew to like the dog, because I knew what she meant to my mother.

Years later, I came to understand my father better. I realised that, growing up under the repressive apartheid system, reduced to a 'boy' by whites because of the colour of his skin, my father's only outlet was to exert his power and authority at home – to the point of harshness. Our relationship did thaw over the years. My mother always said that no one was prouder of me than my father. Whenever I was featured on television or in the newspaper, a beaming Lizo Maqoma would share the news with his gathered friends.

But still, resentment towards my father stayed with me for a long time. I blocked many memories as they were too hurtful. It was not until years later that I made peace with the trauma of my childhood. Ultimately, dancing was my healing.

Gregory's mother at work, age 28. She worked as a teller at OK Bazaars.

*Chief Maqoma and his wife Kayti, South Africa,
c. 1869 (photo by William Moore)*

— 3 —
Born into royalty

I firmly believe my fighting spirit was written in the stars, my fate as a dancer and choreographer determined by the universe. Nothing could stop my artistic spirit from rising. The defiance that my great-great grandfather, Chief Jongumsombovu Maqoma, showed when he fought against the British colonialists is the same that courses through my veins. He too clashed with his father, whom he believed pandered to the colonialists.

The number three seems to be lucky in the Maqoma lineage. Chief Maqoma died in 1873; eighty years later, in 1953, my father

Lizo Maqoma was born. I was born exactly a century later, in 1973. We are all connected.

I was that child who always asked questions, something that really annoyed my parents – to the extent that I was banned from saying 'why' to them. The one person I relied on for support in all ways was my paternal grandmother, my Makhulu. She sensed my fighting spirit and eagerness to succeed, and immersed me in the family's traditions and history. She financially supported my education when things were tough for my parents. And she emotionally supported my dancing when others were against it.

I used to think her stories of our ancestor Chief Maqoma were fairy tales – they sounded too dark to be true. She told me that he should have been called King Maqoma, or Inkosi Maqoma, but the colonialists changed his name to Chief Maqoma as they did not want anyone else to be called King or Queen. I set out to find out more about him.

My grandmother understood my deep interest. She gifted me with a book that changed my understanding: Timothy J.

Stapleton's book, *Xhosa Resistance to Colonial Advance*. This book gave me a fuller grasp of our history. In high school, I'd learned about the freedom fighters who were imprisoned on Robben Island for fighting apartheid, but I never knew that my great-great grandfather was one of the earliest prisoners held there. I was enthralled to learn that the South African struggle did not start with the African National Congress. It started with those who fought against the colonial invasion. Maqoma was foremost among them.

Born in 1798, Jongumsombovu Maqoma was the son of King Ngqika of the Rharhabe division of the Xhosa nation, and a commander of the Xhosa forces during the frontier wars against the British. Older brother of Chief Mgolombane Sandile and nephew of King Hintsa, he was famous for his intellect, bravery and skills as a tactician, warrior and leader in the battle against colonial dispossession, fighting a tenacious guerilla campaign against the British from his mountain base in the Waterkloof mountains in the Eastern Cape. Eventually, however, he was captured and imprisoned on Robben Island off the coast of Cape Town, where he would die under mysterious circumstances at the age of 75.

Learning this made me realise how important Makhulu's oral knowledge was, and how it had immensely contributed to our family history. It was then that I realised the power of storytelling. We no longer tell our stories sitting under a tree or around the fire; we write our stories down so they can be accessed by many more people.

This is what I wanted to do: tell my stories through song and dance. Many years later, I would celebrate the life of my extraordinary ancestor in my own way.

*Chief Jongumsobomvu Maqoma
(c. 1798 – 9 September 1873), National Library
of South Africa*

*Gregory and his brothers
at Langa's wedding, September 2018
From left: Mncedisi, Greg, Langa and Nathi*

— 4 —
Growing up in Soweto

Growing up in Soweto under the apartheid government was a bittersweet experience. It was a tough world and all about survival. Either you made it or you perished.

Local leaders called for stay-aways and consumer boycotts as a strategy to defy the apartheid government and cause economic damage, but this disrupted learning. With the army and police roaming the townships and schools, rubber bullets and tear gas were daily occurrences. Students made it clear that freedom came before education; for the most part, there was no schooling. In extreme instances, soldiers were actually in our classrooms, guns pointing at us, policing whether teachers were feeding us the set curriculum or teaching what the government ironically called anti-apartheid 'propaganda'.

But the system was on its last legs; the government was under huge pressure from the international community. The figure of Nelson Mandela was electrifying. For the longest time, he'd been an enigma – I'd only recently learned about him. As a banned person, no one knew what he looked like: the apartheid government was hell-bent on suppressing any talk of him, and no pictures of him were available to the public. But now, songs created in the townships cried out for his release from jail and the unbanning of the African National Congress. International calls for Mandela's release also intensified, and sanctions were crippling the economy.

Some political parties, fearful of a democratic South Africa, sowed disinformation and violence in the black community. The government flooded the townships with guns and ammunition, supplying these anti-democratic forces.

(These weapons are still a menace in our crime-ridden society, as they remain in the wrong hands.)

In spite of these hardships, Soweto was then, as now, a kaleidoscope of cultural diversity and a Mecca for Black entertainment. There were established singers like Miriam Makeba and her contemporaries, as well as youth groups springing up on every corner of the township, using music to escape the brutality of their lives under apartheid. Musicals like *Umoja* and *Sarafina* were popular in Soweto. Music was a way for people to tell their own stories, and to tell the world the truth about what was happening in South Africa.

My home was close to one of the many hostels in Soweto. The hostel dwellers were migrant workers from all over Southern Africa. There was never a day that these men were not singing and dancing in traditional dress, in groups formed along ethnic lines. Beyond the euphoria of movement, dance was a way for them to remember home and those they'd left behind; it was for survival.

Even though these men were dancing away the sorrow of their displacement, for me it was a wonderful thing to experience, fuelling my love of song and dance. It was through these impromptu performances that I learned about different genres like mbaqanga, maskanda and isicathamiya.

Years later, when I created my dance piece *Beautiful Me*, I was thinking about those Soweto hostel dwellers who inspired me as a boy: the vision of their muscular figures, dripping with sweat, has never left me.

Television was introduced in 1976 in South Africa. I was too little then to understand its true significance, but it became a part of my daily life when I was older. My life was flooded with pop icons like Michael Jackson, George Michael and Prince. The incomparable Brenda Fassie was the local favourite, churning out hit after hit. I wanted to be like them; dress, dance and perform like them. A star! Michael Jackson was a particularly inspirational figure: this was the first time that I saw a black man portrayed in the media in a positive light. That was the beginning of my path into choreography and dance, though I did not realise it at the time.

As a teenager, at home on the weekends, we listened to my father's collection of jazz and soul records: Ella Fitzgerald, Nat King Cole, Cassandra Wilson, Billie Holiday, Nina Simone. I'd listen quietly to the discussions and arguments between my father and his friends: it seemed the more jazz-musician names you could drop, the more respect you earned. My father protected his record collection, keeping the discs in a dedicated space in his bedroom, where I wasn't allowed to touch them without his permission.

My education continued to be disrupted by stay-away calls – and my father was not amused. He wanted me to focus on my studies despite the political turmoil. But it was dangerous to be at school; I remember coming home one day because the police had dispersed young rioters with tear gas and water cannons. Surprisingly, my father was home, standing at the gate reading the *Sowetan*, his daily dose of news. I was excited to talk about Mandela – but it was bad timing on my part. My father was not in a good mood. I don't remember him grabbing me by my white school shirt, but I do remember dangling in the air. My father's moods were always unpredictable, but in this instance, I was at a loss as to what I'd done wrong.

'You do not talk about Nelson Mandela in this house, do you hear me?' my father said, enraged, as he dropped me to the ground. 'You either go to school to study or you end up in prison like those prisoners you love so much!'

'Ewe Tata,' I responded, dazed and in tears.

'You do not bring politics into this house. I take you to school so that you don't end up in prison like Mandela!'

I sobbed and nodded.

'Are you listening to me? Do you hear me?'

Finally he led me into the house. I anticipated a hiding, but instead he ordered me to sit.

'My son.'

'Tata.'

'This country is in the hands of people who never cared about you or me. The only help I can give you is education. I am asking you to stay away from the politics and focus on your schoolwork. Can you do that for me?'

All I could do was apologise again.

Gregory with his aunt, Yalezwa Makana (centre), and cousins at his 17th birthday celebration

Gregory's Makhulu, Cecelia Maqoma

— 5 —
Finding my spirit

I was lucky enough to be close to both my grandmothers when growing up in Soweto. They adored me and I had a wonderful connection with them both. My love for Makhulu – my paternal grandmother – deepened further when she started travelling with me from Soweto every school holiday to her home in picturesque Port Alfred in the Eastern Cape. It was at that time that I developed a passion for travel.

I always looked forward to these trips. Port Alfred is known as Port Manzini to the locals, from the isiXhosa word for water, 'amanzi'. Here lies the famous Kowie River

– although that beautiful river is now a playground of the rich and famous, with seaview apartments, hotels and houses that cost an arm and a leg.

Makhulu devoted her life to community service, as a schoolteacher and later as a psychiatric nurse. She was a much-loved member of the community and one of the bravest women of her generation. My grandmother was working at Fort England Psychiatric Hospital in Makhanda, about an hour's drive from Port Alfred, when I first went to visit her at age 12. She'd coordinate her leave days with my school holidays but would still be called to attend to emergencies; sometimes she would take me with her. She insisted on driving herself in her old jalopy, a blue Toyota Corolla. She would stay over in Grahamstown and only drive home on the weekend to Port Alfred where she lived to limit the exposure to rough mountainous terrain.

I really cherished these trips. I always found peace driving with her. During these drives I was reminded what a great storyteller my Makhulu was. For example: between Port Alfred and Makhanda lies the small town of Bathurst – where you will find the world biggest man-made pineapple, standing 16.5m high with three storeys, an unmissable landmark. My grandmother told me how European settlers for years tried to plant crops in the land around Bathurst, with no success. She said it was our ancestors refusing to give in to colonial powers, denying them the fertility of our land. But the ancestors were tricked; the settlers planted strange new crops, one being pineapple. I chuckled at the thought of ancestors been 'tricked' – but my heart also sank to hear how the land was taken. Was what I'd learned in history class really true?

I turned to her for confirmation. 'But Mama, my history teacher says land was exchanged for European clothing and other things that we did not have?'

She quickly reprimanded me: 'No textbook can teach you about yourself. All that is you is in your blood. Your great, great, great, great grandparents fought for the land and many perished – and we owe it to them to take it back.'

My grandmother lived a very independent

life in the absence of my late grandfather, Wengu Maqoma, descendant of Chief Maqoma. 'Your grandfather loved women, so I left him. We were living in the house that you and your parents are staying in, in Johannnesburg. I returned to the Eastern Cape in Port Alfred to rebuild my life,' she told me.

I think now about what it would have taken for a black woman in 1970s South Africa, at the peak of apartheid, to make that decision – to leave a home and a husband to start again – and actually act on it. I remain in awe of her strength and bravery.

Going to church was part of the holiday package when I was in Port Alfred. When I was in Joburg, my aunt Nosizwe would take me to St John's Anglican Church in Orlando East, where I was baptised and received my confirmation. But though I frequented church, I had many deepening questions about Christianity. Why was Sunday the dedicated day; why did I have special shoes, the best shoes, for church? Why did you need to look a certain way to have a relationship with God? My Christian background meant that I never believed in ancestral worship, a topic that was alluded to in church as evil.

When I was 19, I left my aunt's home. It was then that I made it a mission to understand my own identity – and tapped into my family's ancestral history for answers. I needed to do something different to awaken my own spirit. And dance was already there: a way to awaken the fire that lives inside all of us.

Gregory and Vincent Mantsoe as independent artists

— 6 —
A brotherhood of Trust

I have always been lucky enough to be surrounded by people who are passionate about what they do, even if some of them did not share my passion for dance. I have built friendships that have stood the test of time.

As a teenager, I was still searching for my own identity. Wanting to fit in, and influenced by the trends of the time, I tried all sorts of things, like dressing differently. But still, I felt there was no one who really understood me, who had the same needs as mine. Until I met Vincent. Vincent Mantsoe is one of my closest friends. Our bond, a brotherhood of trust, spans more than three decades. Built on mutual respect, it flourished through dance.

Making friendships as a kid in the 1980s was not easy. You had to choose your friends carefully, because of political instability and the presence of gangs. A 'friend' might end up betraying you to authorities, or else luring you into a gang, which was a death wish. Survival was everything. Escape was a way of life in those days – literally by jumping fences, running away from live police bullets and tear gas, or figuratively through song and dance.

When Vincent and I met we were 14 years old, in our first year at Bona Secondary School in Orlando East. I grew up in Orlando East, identifiable by its orange bricks, and Vincent in Diepkloof, with its rusty-black bricks – all houses built by the government and referred to by the community as 'matchboxes', given their size. But we saw each other almost daily, brought together by the love of dance.

He immediately struck me as different: there was an distinctive aura about him that piqued my curiosity. I had joined the local drum majorettes, where I played the big drum. My discipline was honed during this period: not only was I learning how to play drums, but also teaching girls new moves and routines, without even knowing I was already dealing with choreography. Although I enjoyed it, it was draining: there were long drives to far-away parades for funeral send-offs for comrades killed in political violence. I met Vincent at this time.

Vincent was just as passionate about dance as I was. In the midst of the chaos of a township adolescence, we recruited three other young men to form a pop street-dance group, the Joy Dancers. We embraced popular contemporary American dance routines, mixing them with South African urban rhythms and styles. In particular, we wanted to replicate popular African American boy bands like the Jackson 5, The Temptations and New Edition.

The Joy Dancers performed at weddings, concerts and dance competitions. Though many enjoyed our performances, we were also met with scepticism and judgement: young boys in colourful shirts and torn, stonewashed jeans was not a sight that township dwellers at the time were used to. These were the marks of the township 'punk' subculture: we tinted our hair, cut our pants to three-quarters length. We wanted to be seen!

At school, we also had to fight for space and for our identity. We were called the 'Michael Jackson plastics' and seen as unruly. And this always confused me, because we felt vulnerable, isolated and alone at school as we were bullied daily, and subjected to various forms of humiliation. For example, we had to pay a protection fee to some of the seniors, resulting in us skipping school: between the bullies and the army, it wasn't the best place for us.

Every weekend, the Joy Dancers walked to Diepkloof to practise dance moves in the backyard of Vincent's family home. Vincent's father allowed us to use his expensive vinyl player and radio-tape deck. These provided good sound for our dance moves. The first hour of practice was spent sprinkling the ground with water to reduce the amount of dust we raised.

Our first assignment as a group was to put together a dance routine for a local dance competition. We chose a song from the pop group Wham. But while George Michael's group was popular, our song selection was a little unusual: the lesser-known track 'Blue' from the album *Music from the Edge of Heaven*. It was a taste of the aesthetic we were creating: connected to the popular culture, but with the added zest of something unique.

Over the weekends, when weren't rehearsing or performing as the Joy Dancers, I was either at church or on the road with the drum majorettes. But Vincent participated in the rituals that were practised by the women in his family, including his mother, who were traditional healers. These rites, too, involved song and dance.

My other great childhood friend, Tebogo Letsitsi, was a consummate reader. He immersed himself in academics in high school. Tebogo initially discouraged me from becoming a dancer, but later he became one of the biggest supporters of my art.

I met Tebogo when we were in grade 4, when we found ourselves sharing a desk at Ditau Higher Primary school. We gravitated towards each other, even sharing our lunch boxes. I'd visit his home after school, as he lived close to a library and a post office where I would pick up the allowance my grandmother sent me every month from Port Alfred.

We spent a lot of time in the library: Tebogo loved books. As primary students we enjoyed reading Danielle Steel; I'd take a long time, but Tebogo could finish a book in a week. Then he'd want to discuss, so I had to catch up quickly! Tebogo lived with his grandmother, a retired teacher, and an aunt who was referred to as Mom Mthobi, a gentle woman who took us all in. Tebogo's home was modest, but beautifully furnished, and had high walls compared to mine and most houses in Soweto. That's how he got the nickname 'Mthangala' – 'High Walls'.

We both got good grades and were often singled out by the principal as high achievers. Wednesdays were a technical day for the boys – we'd be bused to a workshop for woodwork, technical drawing and electrical skills. Tebogo and I hated it; we asked the principal if we could do something different and came up with the idea of planting trees on the school grounds instead. The principal understood that we were a little bit different, that we were vulnerable and needed protection from the bullying we were already experiencing. We were called 'softies', though we did not really understand what that meant. I'm happy to say our tree project was very successful; to this day, every time I pass the school I see how big and beautiful our trees have grown.

Tebogo and I started high school together, opting for the same science subjects so we could stick together. We got bullied even more at high school, due to our softness and cleanliness and how we held ourselves. Being among the top learners in the school also quickly made us a target for bullies. Our teachers protected us where possible, but challenges awaited us on the way home, outside the school perimeter.

We attended Saturday school at Wits University, and afterwards would catch movies at the Carlton Centre in the Johannesburg CBD. I think it was during this time that we both started questioning our sexualities, although we never talked about it directly. It was totally taboo and unacceptable in our community.

We both applied to Wits – I hoping to study medicine, and Tebogo a BSc – but it was not to be. Tebogo did his BSc, and later an MBA at Rhodes University, while I went to the Gordon Institute of Business Science (GIBS) to study social entrepreneurship. (It would have made me smile to know then that today I am a case study at GIBS – their MBA students often visit my studios in Newtown.) For the first time my friend and I were separated, exploring life along different paths. Four years later we reunited, comfortable in our skins and able to speak openly about our sexuality. We remain very close friends to this day, celebrating our achievements and differences.

Sometimes, Tebogo teases me, reminding me how I used to bunk school for dance classes in primary school. Then I remind him that he wrote and directed a play back then, starring me in the lead role – so he is also responsible for my love of the stage, and the path my life has taken.

Gregory with his childhood friends, Shakes Mokgosi, Vincent Mantsoe and Tebogo Letsitsi

*An injured Gregory, supported
by Sylvia Glasser of Moving into Dance*

– 7 –
Moving into dance

In 1990, I was in Grade 11. My relationship with my father was still fraught. As the oldest son, I was to carry the family name forward with dignity. Men were supposed to be doctors, lawyers, schoolteachers – or soccer stars. My love of the arts was a huge embarrassment to my father. But it was in my father's *Sowetan* that I saw the advertisement calling for young people to be trained in dance. I knew it was for me. I took Vincent along and encouraged him to audition too.

Moving into Dance was a non-racial dance training company started by cultural activist Sylvia Glasser in the late 1970s, at the height of apartheid. Sylvia says she remembers me as an intelligent, bright young man. She's kind enough to say that my beauty, poise and confidence distinguished me from the rest of the group. Vincent and I were both accepted by Moving into Dance and offered a one-year scholarship; I joined as a part-time student.

My ever-supportive mother understood what this opportunity meant to me. We made a pact to keep it a secret from my father – but it didn't take long for him to find out, when a picture of me dancing appeared in the newspaper. Much to my surprise, he wasn't angry. He opened his arms and gave me a warm embrace. Seeing my success, with my name in the pages of his beloved *Sowetan*, no less, had helped him to accept my choice of life direction.

When I completed my matric in 1991, my parents had no money to send me to university. I wanted to study medicine, but there were few to no scholarships for black youngsters. I applied to study Moving into Dance's Community Teachers Training Course, which would enable me to teach dance in schools across Soweto. Sylvia Glasser taught us how to 'edu-dance' – teaching township children the alphabet through dance during our outreach sessions. I enjoyed working with young people, and seeing my work blossom through them. I may not have become a medical doctor as my parents wished, but in this way I touched many lives.

I got my first taste of international travel with Moving into Dance. In 1992, apartheid was dying and South Africa was transitioning into a democratic state. To save face, the National Party was pretending to the world that it was embracing democracy and non-racialism. They funded the racially diverse cast of Moving into Dance to take part in the World Expo in Sevilla, Spain.

I remember my first time out of the country as an out-of-body experience. I was only 19 years old, and this was the biggest arts gathering I'd ever seen. The venue was palatial and packed with art displays from across the globe. Every country had its own pavilion displaying their crafts. I remember seeing the Statue of Liberty display, part of the United States' expo, and dreamed of visiting one day. I knew right then that I wanted to travel the world.

However, dancing and teaching weren't paying enough for me to make a living, and I was still dependent on my parents. And then suddenly that relationship was reversed: when my mother lost her job and my father was retrenched, I had to take care of them. So I left dancing in 1994 to work in the insurance business. I was placed with an Afrikaans company, where the language barrier was a huge challenge for me; I stood little chance of succeeding. In any event, I found the idea of sitting behind a desk all day deeply uninspiring. The job was killing me.

More importantly, the dancing bug never left me alone. I kept on dancing on weekends. Vincent, however, was far more advanced: he'd started to create work driven by the spiritual practices he grew up with. His work was gaining international acclaim and winning awards. In 1996, Vincent's piece won first prize at Dance Encounters of Contemporary African Dance, the first African dance competition supported by the French government. The prize included an eight-country African tour package.

Vincent knew my frustration at work, and he knew my love for dance went beyond a monthly cheque. I was hugely moved when he invited me to join him on tour – and on the road back to professional dance. In many ways, he rescued me.

I promptly left my job. My passion for dance was re-invigorated. I knew then that there was nothing else I wanted to do in life except dance; it was and is my calling.

Gregory with his parents at his farewell lunch before leaving to study in Brussels on a scholarship

With the Moving into Dance team
From left: Gcina Grace Mkhize, the late Portia Mashigo,
Themba Nkabinde, Angelina Sekonya, Keke Lehana,
Gregory, Zakhele Nkosi and Pule Kgaratsi

— 8 —
An African odyssey

I never tire of talking about my first experience of travel. Moving into Dance was the first South African dance company to travel through Africa, engaging with our peers in Kenya, Ghana, Angola, Congo and Nigeria. I was one of eight dancers on the tour: six young men and two young women.

On that trip, I fell head over heels in love with Africa. Having grown up in a country where being black was a sin, it was a revelation to discover other parts of the continent: In the sea of black faces, I saw myself in on every street corner. I got a sense of what Ghana's first president, Kwame Nkrumah, meant when he spoke of the dream of a united Africa.

My first experience of open-air theatre was in Accra, Ghana, where we performed as part of the Alliance Française programme. The atmosphere was vibrant and warm, the ocean breeze welcoming as we presented my friend Vincent's award-winning *Gula Matari* and Sylvia Glasser's *Stone Cast Ritual*.

The latter piece, a ritual procession, required absolute discipline. The dancers each carried a pair of stones, which they rhythmically beat together. The work is meant to be meditative, like tai chi, every movement calculated with care and grace. But our dance quickly became a spectacle as we were attacked by mosquitoes as big as flies, attracted by our semi-naked, sweaty bodies and the bright lights of the theatre – it was war! They seemed to be biting us in time to the dance, because all eight of us were shooing them away with our stones in perfect synchrony. With every bite, our bodies twitched and trembled as if possessed, our feet stamping in unison, as if this had all been rehearsed. For this we received a standing ovation from the audience, who had no idea what we were going through! As soon as the piece was over, we charged offstage and ran for cold showers.

The streets of Accra were abuzz with energy. At the city's main Makola Market, traders won over customers with their biggest smiles, selling everything from vegetables to printed cloth. On our free days, we went to the beach – Labadi beach, near Teshie, was the most popular. It boasted a large beachfront with lots of space to sit and umbrellas bowing to Accra's warm afternoon sun. A sea view dotted with narrow fishing boats, a shoreline steeped in history, the sound of waves crashing on soft, yellow sand, and at night, bars filling the air with music ... I was 23 years old and I wanted to party! My dear friend Pule Kgaratsi, also part of the company, taught me a lot about that – we missed no opportunity to discover Accra by night, sneaking out of the hotel in spite of all warnings from our hosts about the perils of West African nightlife.

Our last stop was Nigeria. This was a culture shock for the crew. In South Africa's new democracy, bribery and corruption were not everyday occurrences. But things were different here. When one of the dancers refused to pay the police, we all gasped when he received a hard slap. The Nigerian policeman was the biggest man we'd ever seen, and he unleased all his physical might on the youngster, which silenced us immediately. Our tour manager, more experienced in the ways of the world, ended up paying the bribe. And there were other issues. When people learned that we were South African, some sneeringly called us 'Mandela's children' – a dig at what they saw as the weakness of Mandela's agreement with the apartheid regime at the time of the democratic transition.

After that, we couldn't wait to get home. The experience lingered: when we landed in Johannesburg, two days before Christmas, none of us said a word to each other. That's how disappointed we felt. Still, most of the Nigerians we'd met had been incredibly warm and welcoming, as had our other African hosts. The problem lay with the corrupt officials.

On that first trip, I made everlasting friendships that would propel me to new levels of creativity. In Nairobi I met Faustin Linyekula, a self-exiled dancer from Kisangani, a village in the north of the DRC. In 2000 our paths crossed again, when I collaborated with Faustin on *Tales of the Mud Wall*, a piece commissioned by the Tanzwochen Festival in Austria and presented at the Johannesburg Dance Umbrella Festival in 2001. Then in 2006, ten years after we first met, I wanted to create a dance piece that celebrated ancestral lineage. I knew that I needed Africans who were connected to their spirituality, history and place of origin and used dance to celebrate it. Faustin, Vincent and I, along with British choreographer Akram Khan, together developed the piece which became *Beautiful Me*. I was happy to have the opportunity to tour this work in the country of Faustin's birth, the Congo.

Sadly, though, on this trip corruption again raised its head. When I lost my passport, I had to pay endless bribes – twenty dollars to be allowed into the police station; another twenty before the officer would write an affidavit confirming who I was; another twenty to get the affidavit from them. I went to the South African embassy thinking that my troubles were over – but no, it would take three weeks for my new passport to arrive. This meant I'd be left alone in a strange country, as our tour was finishing. I screamed in frustration, 'I am South African! You need to help me! You can't send me out to a war zone!' At last I was flatly told by a Congolese guy that the only way to leave the country was to buy my way out. I parted with US$ 500, paying out a little more at every checkpoint. The irony: the work we were touring, *Beautiful Me*, questioned corruption. And by paying out bribes, I'd become a small part of that system.

In the years since, I've travelled to many other parts of Africa and learned that each corner has its own story to tell. Africa compels you to be a storyteller, and stories are everywhere – and I never tire of telling them through dance.

Vincent Mantsoe, Gregory and Pule Kgaratsi touring with Moving into Dance in the Netherlands, 1990s

The Moving into Dance team with Sylvia Glasser (far left), touring Australia

— 9 —
Losing a father – and finding forefathers

After that first African tour, I continued to teach and work, focusing on community and youth work and honing my craft as a solo artist. But my wanderlust persisted – there were still parts of the world I wanted to see. In 1998, the Performing Arts Research and Training Studios (PARTS), a school for contemporary dance and choreography in Brussels, held auditions in South Africa. I applied, and was granted a scholarship for a three-year BA programme.

The school was a hot spot for recruiters

and scouts from across Europe. I was very committed, always in the studio working, and it paid off. Still a first-year student, I caught the eye of a scout from the Holland International Theatre Festival. This festival only accepted dance pieces from companies, not individuals, so I had to form a company – and that's how Vuyani Dance Theatre was born.

Together with two other South African students at PARTS, Moya Michael and Shanell Winlock, I created *Rhythm 1.2.3* – the first dance piece under the banner of Vuyani Dance Theatre. I wanted to be unapologetic about celebrating Africa and move away from the dark pessimism and self-pity that is so often projected about the continent. An ode to Johannesburg and the complexity of post-apartheid South Africa, *Rhythm 1.2.3* was very well received by international audiences.

My time in Belgium and then the Netherlands laid the groundwork for my international career. It was a period of incredible artistic growth, both for myself and for African dance. The world was opening up to a new wave of creatives who would go on to shape the next two decades of contemporary dance.

But even so, my place in South African theatre was a work in progress when I returned from Europe from the scholarship. Local theatres did not think that dance would sell – especially as such performances were an unfamiliar experience for many black South Africans, who'd been cut off from cultural resources and institutions during apartheid. Joburg Theatre in particular was a tough nut to crack – but Vuyani Dance Theatre broke that barrier when, in 2014, it brought the first contemporary Black choreography to that venue; it was also the first South African Black dance company to present a season on the theatre's main Mandela stage.

From the start, international audiences had a lot of interest in my work, and they remained enthusiastic. The audiences that propelled me to stardom and filled theatres for my work was mainly in European countries, where dance and theatre were long established and taught. Back in South Africa, I continued to get invitations from France and other European countries. And I made more new work all the time, because I knew there would always be support in that part of the world.

As Vuyani Dance Theatre gained respect, the founding members, myself and Shanell Winlock Pailman, were building a reputation as a ground-breaking duo who pushed theatrical boundaries. One of our first significant works was *Southern Comfort*, which premiered in London in 2001 as part of the Celebrate South Africa Festival, under the eye of then UK South African High Commissioner, Cheryl Carolus. It was at this festival that I connected with British choreographer Akram Khan, who invited Shanell to join his company. Shanell and I maintained our connection and where possible would perform together. Shanell now works with Vuyani as movement analyst, mentor, dramaturgist and choreographer. Our friendship and collaboration over the years has been amply rewarded with awards for dance and choreography.

In 2009, on the crest of this wave of success, I was on a residency at Bates College in Maine, teaching and developing work. It was a beautiful summer morning, and I'd woken to seven missed calls, some from numbers I did not recognise. Outside, the early birds were serenading me. Looking at these odd numbers, my heart rate sped up and the hair on my arms rose. I felt like a ghost was moving through my space. I thought at once of my grandmother, who was ailing.

I tried to push away my feeling of foreboding. Sitting on my bed, I started to plan my class for the day. Soon my thoughts were absorbed in the work, dance sequences building in my mind. Then the phone rang again, one of the unrecognised numbers shining brightly on the screen.

I answered, but could only get to 'hello' before the call cut off. I sank back on my bed, unsettled, my mind running like it does when something is not completely accomplished, or my creative ideas are not coming together. I decided to use my long-distance call card, which I usually used to call my mother. On the line, I heard my 17-year-old brother's voice – but he wasn't paying attention. Multiple voices were in the background, cries of men and women and a dog barking, which I recognised as my mother's dog. In the commotion I dropped the call, worried that I'd run out of credit without establishing what was going on. I dialled the second number on the list of missed calls.

'Who is this?' said a voice. It was my young cousin Zanele. In the background, the same voices and cries. 'Greg is that you, Mamela – listen, Papa Lizo passed on ...'

At that moment, all sounds ceased. The breath left my lungs.

'Greg? Are you there?'

Nothing but silence; nothing but the sound of birds in the trees outside.

My father was gone.

I travelled home to bury him with dignity, and to be there for my mother and siblings. I did not want to carry the burden of not burying my father: as the new head of the family, and in Xhosa tradition, the expectation was that I would lead the proceedings. I was also the family's sole breadwinner. I comforted myself with the thought that in the end, I had become the strong heir my father wanted me to be, even though it was not through a medium he deemed worthy.

I thought about my father's passing, and how he died without leaving an inheritance. It made me think more seriously about my own legacy. And this is what led me back to my grandmother's old stories – and to the figure of my illustrious ancestor, Chief Maqoma.

Gregory's father, late 1990s

Gregory dancing in Exit/Exist
(photo by Arthur Dlamini)

10

Exit/Exist

My ancestor Chief Maqoma prophesied that he would never be at peace – that even if the colonists killed him, his bones would rise up and fight. A century later, these words were borne out.

In 1978, Chief Maqoma's spirit visited a seer called Nomantombi 'Charity' Sonandi to inform her that his bones were not resting easily. She accurately described in detail where his remains would be found on Robben Island. Maqoma's collarbone would have a bullet hole in it, she said, showing that he had indeed been murdered. Hearing this, the family, under the leadership of Chief Lent Maqoma and his councillors, decided to exhume the bones.

The day they were due to sail to Robben Island was windy and cold. At Cape Town harbour, the rough sea lashed the shoreline, making it almost impossible for the Chief's party to take the boat to the island. But despite the danger, there was no turning back. They braved the seas. On the island, they were directed to a secluded area where there were many unmarked graves. Here, the seer performed her ritual, invoking divine powers. As it began to rain, she stood on top of one of the graves and declared: 'This is it, this is him.'

The councillors dug down to the bones. Everything in the seer's vision was accurate – the fatal bullet hole was clearly visible. The body was indeed the chief, son of Ngcika. Chief Maqoma's remains were duly exhumed and reburied in 1978 in the Ciskei at Ntaba ka Ndoda (Great Place of the Xhosa kings).

Inspired by my ancestor's epic journey and return, I wanted to create a dance piece to honour the spirit of Chief Maqoma, to preserve his name and spirit, his fight for land and human dignity. To symbolise the flow of his blood, and the blood of the ancestors who came before him. I envisioned a performance in which golden oil covered my body: his spirit would sparkle among the stars. *Exit/Exist* would be an auto-ethnographic exploration challenging the systematic, violent erasure of our history – mine and that of the Black South African nation.

But first I had to follow protocol. My cousin Loyiso Maqoma, filmmaker, writer and son of Lent Maqoma, learned of my intentions to make a dance work about Chief Maqoma. He contacted me to caution me about the power of the Chief's spirit. I would need to go to his grave and ask for his blessings before I could tell his tale. And so in 2011 I made the journey to the Eastern Cape.

Loyiso gathered the family elders at his father's farm. As per tradition, the men gathered at the cattle kraal to talk to the ancestors, alerting them of my intentions and introducing me to my heritage. The moment was extraordinary. I was so moved by the stories told by my elders, which confirmed those told to me by my grandmother. I am often overpowered by emotion when I dance, but standing there in the kraal, calling on my ancestors to be with me, outside the safe confines of a theatre, was a transcendental moment in my life.

I felt welcomed by my blood elders. Their faces and bodies spoke of the hard lives of men who worked the land; and they carried in them the pain of Chief Maqoma, who died yearning for the land taken by force. 'The story of Chief Maqoma is bigger than all of us combined,' one of the elders remarked. A sheep was slaughtered as a gift to the ancestors and lunch was served to get us ready for the hour-long drive to the grave of Chief Maqoma.

On the way, we encountered a massive storm. Gusty winds forced the convoy of cars to pull to the side of the road. I was in Loyiso's car. Should we go back or continue? We have an expression, 'Indlela ibuzwa kwabaphambili', which means: 'Those who have gone before are the ones who can show the path.' So it was important to follow the elders' guidance in this mission. Loyiso took out his phone and called one of the elders at the head of the convoy.

'It is Chief Maqoma,' came the response. 'Uvela ngesivunguvungu,' – he appears in a form of a whirlwind. And so: 'Siyaphambili!' We carry on.

We drove on into the tempest – with me at times holding my breath in fear. In the storm, I felt Chief Maqoma's loneliness and anger. Was this his way of saying he was with us? Maybe a welcome? Or perhaps a sign that he was disappointed, expecting more from us?

Eerily, the weather calmed as soon as we got to his grave. We stood there under a tiny umbrella, heads bowed. The leading elder started with clan praises, then introduced me to my ancestor. I moved forward, and spoke to Chief Maqoma with rain falling like tears down my face. I asked for his permission to raise his name through my work, to take his name to the world. When I was done, the rain stopped abruptly. The elder turned towards me. 'Uvumile,' he said. He has agreed.

Under the direction of James Ngcobo and with a musical composition by Simphiwe Dana, I created and choreographed *Exit/Exist*, the dance piece exploring my family history and my experience as a descendant of Chief Maqoma. The piece premiered in 2012 in Johannesburg at the Market Theatre. We decided to bus in audiences from the townships – people who'd never been to a theatre before. Many of them were hesitant; but once they were there, they changed their minds about what theatre represents. The piece has since played in over 100 cities around the world. I could not be prouder to fulfil my ancestor's promise to rise again, and to aid in the spiritual return of an exceptional leader who sacrificed his life for his people.

In Exit/Exist, *Gregory as Chief Maqoma asks, 'Where are the cattle?' (photo by Arthur Dlamini)*

The Moving into Dance team going on tour for the first time with Pule Kgaratsi, Vincent Mantsoe and Gregory, 1992

— 11 —
Becoming me

Some people are more than just friends; they're family. I developed an incredible bond with my friend Pule – but our friendship was never without drama! I met him one cold winter morning in 1990: my audition day at Moving Into Dance at the Braamfontein Recreation Centre. Pule was in colourful tights and a vest that showed his well-developed body. He was the centre of attention – you couldn't take your eyes off him.

The audition was conducted by Bev Elgie, an amazing teacher who warmed to me and dedicated time in class to my growth. I am forever grateful for those foundation days.

Bev and I became close, and she introduced me to her family. Her husband, renowned actor Graham Hopkins, helped me with maths and science when I was in Grade 12.

During a break in auditions, I was in the changeroom, nursing my nerves and pacing the room. Pule walked in and introduced himself with a handshake. I responded with a smile, and cautiously offered that I thought I was doing alright in the auditions. Indeed, we both made it through – and that was the start of a life-changing friendship.

Pule was older, clearly more experienced, and a dresser of note – always impeccable in designer clothes. He was in his first year of dancing, finishing his teaching diploma and ready to taste the world out there. A year later, Pule was teaching at a private school; a number of my newly found friends in Pimville, where I lived with my aunt, were learners there. They told me how strict he was at school – something we'd laugh about when I met him at our dance classes.

I was only 17 when I met Pule, and still figuring out my sexuality. I had many mixed feelings, and often hated the thoughts going through my mind. I tried dating girls, but soon lost interest. I spent three years in denial, forced into a dark corner – to the extent of having suicidal thoughts. It was my friendship with Pule that helped me through this difficult time. Pule took me to my first gay club, Skyline in Hillbrow – an experience that opened my eyes. It was the first time I really encountered the gay community. As much as it was a revelation, it was also damn scary!

Pule and I soon decided to share a two-bedroom apartment in Yeoville. He was a teacher and I was working for the insurance company, so we had some income. During the time we lived together, I became more and more comfortable with my sexuality – slowly opening up and becoming more self-accepting. When Pule and I toured with Moving into Dance, we'd always share a hotel room. And we partied hard, on tour and at home. While we were never lovers, we were inseparable friends – which made it difficult for the people we dated; the bond was too strong to let anyone in. He was always the one to defend me in confrontations with others; the brother ready to stand up and fight for me.

My gay family, many of whom were in the same artistic field, was growing: it felt comfortable and reassuring. Pule became a trusted family friend. Both my parents took a liking to him and he attended every family gathering; I also got to meet his family. Unfortunately, he lost both of parents when he was young, something that he didn't like to talk about. I met his sister, who was like a mother to him, and grew close to his nephews, nieces and the whole extended family.

Then, one cold winter day in 2017, 30 July, my phone rang. I was in Cape Town, working on a production of *King Kong*. I was in a car with a group of friends, going for an afternoon chisa nyama (barbecue) in Langa township. On the phone was Pule's long-time partner, Reginald 'Tsalo' Mahibila, whom I'd been friends with for as long as I'd known Pule. Tsalo was crying, hysterical; I pulled the car over to make sense of the call. I heard him say Pule had died ... the words echoed. I blacked out.

I was brought back to reality by questions from my friends in the car – what happened?

Greg, what's wrong?

I stepped out of the car.

Pule has died.

I was in total disbelief. He'd been doing so well: just appointed as the first black principal at Sandown High School in Sandton. He'd also just moved to a new apartment at Eye of Africa, where we'd all said we wanted to retire, and got engaged to Tsalo. How could he die, when everything was going so well?

Pule was brutally shot and killed in Soweto. The motive is still not known; the police let the case go cold. I still feel the void he left. First, denial and shock. Then, a pain that would not go away – and an anger I'm still not sure how to get past.

The last theatrical work of mine that Pule watched was *Cion: Requiem Of Ravel's Bolero*, set in a graveyard. It ends with a procession, evoking death, mourning, redemption, rebirth. I danced the lead. He was the first to rise to his feet when the curtain fell.

Now I see, looking back, that that production was a last lament for my dear friend. I was never able to perform that work again after his passing – but I have amplified its message of grief in my subsequent work. All part of my attempt to soothe the long pain of Black experience; the pain that makes us all professional mourners.

Gregory's dear friend and brother, the late Pule Kgaratsi

ZO! MUTE, *a work that came out of the continued silencing of whistleblowers (photo by Arthur Dlamini)*

— 12 —
Choreography: A passion like no other

My life choices have often been unconventional. Dance was an unusual and in many ways challenging choice for someone from my background: a Black child brought up in Soweto in the 1980s, in a middle-class, Christian family that looked on education as a stepping stone to the Promised Land. I have reached the pinnacle of my career, performing in cities across the world, but dance remains a difficult vocation. Even today, when I introduce myself as a dancer, I usually get a follow-on question – 'so what else do you do?'

The answer is: I dance!

Still, I have never stopped believing in my craft, even when times were tough. As a dancer and choreographer, I don't think I have a formula: I allow an idea to haunt me until I have no choice but to bring it to life. Yes, there is a thought process and choices made, but I allow what comes naturally, in the moment, to take precedence. And always, I work hand in hand with many gifted colleagues.

A dance piece is made of many parts. The audience sees a beautiful ensemble, but often are unaware of the diverse skills and talents it takes to put together a show. The choreographer works with designers, composers, set designers, lighting designers, programmers and others. Just putting together outfits for each performance is a formidable task: every outfit must reflect the mood and narrative the choreographer creates. Actors and dancers extend that narrative. It's a group effort at every stage.

I understood this from early on. When I started dancing, it was in a group. My time with the drum majorettes taught me the power of collaboration, and when I created my first professional choreographed piece in 1994, it was for a trio. (That piece was for the Moving Into Dance Young Dancers Program, and won me my first award.) In fact, most of my work has been for ensemble pieces; such performances feel like an extension of myself, with others as witnesses to my craft. My mission is to connect on a spiritual level to the people I work with, a connection that is not always possible to explain in earthly words. I rely on my intuition when choosing my dance team. It is that heightened spiritual appreciation that drives the integrity of my collaborative process.

This sense of community extends well beyond the company: my dance pieces are always connected to Africa and its people. African spirituality plays a big role. I work a lot with dreams, which traditional healers say are communications from ancestral spirits. I find myself invoking the spirit in my work – the sangoma dances manifest in my body, and can call to the spirit in those watching. I guess it runs in the family:

these days, my brother Langa doesn't only heal the sick but also helps new initiates to achieve their gifts, and our house is known as a home for sangomas.

I see a dance studio as a church, a place of worship, a place I can connect with God and my ancestors. In this spirit, I created Vuyani Dance Theatre; and while it began in Europe, my dream was always to build an African space to develop our stories. A place to turn communities' disadvantage into advantage. My vision came to me when I was an outsider in Europe – but also looking at South Africa from the outside as the country transitioned from apartheid to democracy.

I love community work. I was made in the community and by the community, and dance speaks to that, raising awareness about social issues like sexual assault and domestic violence. At Vuyani, we hold community sessions in Soweto, mentoring young, aspiring dancers. During Vuyani Week Season, we create a programme of dance with these outreach groups, where they get to perform with the company. This event brings families together and is a community favourite.

Vuyani Dance Theatre has broken barriers, and I am proud of that. But I am prouder of the difference the company has made to the lives and livelihoods of the people who are part of it, from trainees to management. Nothing makes me happier than knowing that my company, directly or indirectly, has contributed to the careers of so many. It is particularly fulfilling to see my protégés – Luyanda Sidiya, Lulu Mlangeni and many others – taking on leadership roles and writing their own histories.

I have also given my all for family. I have a 21-year-old son, who came into my life when he was three and lived with me pretty much throughout his childhood. His father and I were in a relationship for 15 years. I realised when I first held my son that there was no turning back from the decision, that I would be a role model and a part of what he turned out to be. I dedicated my time and resources to ensuring that he never missed out on an opportunity to be a child, and that he enjoyed his upbringing.

In turn, my son changed my life; my

undying love for him has brought so much gentleness into my existence, and taught me so many lessons about humanity. He is a constant reminder that investment in people is far more important than the glitz and glamour this industry often promises. Currently, he is in the USA, on a culinary apprenticeship after completing three years of culinary art studies in South Africa. He sends me music compilations; we remain very close.

When my brother Langa had his first child, he asked me to give him a name. I wanted the name to honour my father and those who came before him. I am very intentional in the naming of children: I believe a name carries power, resonating with the energy of the person named. For this child I chose 'Akhona', a unisex name, which means 'the presence of all blessings in abundance; the one born free'. He too is under my care, and blossoming.

I love my country. I've always been an incurable optimist; even growing up in dusty Soweto, suffocating from teargas, I believed in the good of people. But walking the streets of Soweto today, I see the younger generation in the streets, hopeless, with no spaces for recreation, no stimulus – no art, except on the street-corners, always under tremendous strain. This has motivated me: the last two decades of my career have been about creating a space for the Black child to be inspired. I believe that the arts should be a part of every school curriculum, to teach young people about humanity and the resilience of the human spirit. Experimenting with the arts at a young age creates the artistic geniuses of tomorrow, in dance and every other genre.

Leaving a lasting legacy in my community is my greatest passion. I understand how difficult it is for young Black people to get into spaces that are not traditionally considered theirs. Even though things have changed since my day, it is still a challenge in townships for the arts to flourish. This is why I want to leave a legacy by a building a space; all the theatres I've performed in have inspired me so much. I want to inspire Black children and give them a creative space where they can flourish, be inspired, and know that they have a home; I want them to be able to see a future for themselves when entering that space.

In my fortieth year, I started thinking about how I would eventually retire. Five years later, I bought myself a piece of land in Henley on Klip, a tranquil neighbourhood to the south of Johannesburg. The land is currently in development as a retirement village, but also as an artists' residency – a place for African artists to think and break bread together, where we can be creative, be allowed to fail, learn from the failures, and count our successes. This is where children will be raised, where love will manifest, a place where I will be writing, dreaming and simply living; and perhaps a place where I will get married.

As artists, we have a huge responsibility. The world faces many crises, from wars to climate change. But I believe creativity is a powerful weapon, our most important tool to navigate the future and find ways to heal. Our collective power can challenge and defeat our current enemies – just as we once defeated the apartheid government with our vision, courage and creativity.

Gregory in New York in 2019 to present Cion: Requiem of Ravel's Bolero, *which resulted in the New York City Bessie Award for Dance*

Photo by Arthur Dlamini

Appendix 1
Theatre productions

Over the last forty years, I have had the privilege of creating numerous dance, musical and theatre productions. There are too many to describe in detail, but here are some that are personal highlights. Among them are works I have created to speak directly to what I see as a need for activism. More than ever, we need art that can speak truth and deepen our consciousness, that can encourage us all to think about the world we live in, and pay far more attention to our degraded planet and humanity.

I am perhaps best known for my trilogies. My early Rhythm Trilogy – made up of

Rhythm 1.2.3 (1999), *Rhythm Blues* (2000) and *Rhythm Colour* (2002) – tapped into the now by reflecting on the past. The Beautiful Trilogy is made up of *Beautiful* (2005 – a duet with Shanell Winlock), the solo *Beautiful Me* (2006) and *Beautiful Us* (2006). It deals with humanity, leadership and the struggle for power in Africa and beyond. *Beautiful Me* shows power as a manifestation of human greed. The solo also concentrates on the relationship I developed with the three co-creators of the piece: Vincent Mantsoe, Faustin Linyekula and Akram Khan. *Beautiful Us* brings our attention to the decay of our planet as humanity turns a blind eye. It tells a story of men digging deep into the belly of the earth, searching for gold they would never own.

In 2010, I was proud to be appointed head choreographer for the FIFA World Cup Kick-Off Concert held in Soweto.

In 2012, my solo work *Exit/Exist* reflected on the memory and legacy of my ancestor, Chief Jongumsobomvu Maqoma. Under the direction of James Ngcobo, I was accompanied on stage by four South African singers and a guitarist. David Tlale's costume and the musical collaboration from Simphiwe Dana, Giuliano Modarelli and IComplete all helped to tell the story.

In 2017, I choreographed British actor and Hollywood heavyweight Idris Elba and Kwame Kwei-Armah's project *Tree*. Idris Elba was riding the wave of his newly released movie, *Long Walk to Freedom*, where he played Nelson Mandela.

In 2018, I performed and choreographed William Kentridge's *The Head and the Load*. The show presents the untold story of the nearly two million Africans who were used as porters by the British, French and Germans in the First World War, bearing the brunt of the casualties. The show boasted an exceptional creative team: renowned artist Kentridge in the director's seat, and Phillip Miller, one of South Africa's leading composers, and Thuthuka Sibisi as co-composers and music directors.

In 2019, I brought celebrated South African author Zakes Mda's novel *Cion* to the stage. I collaborated with Nhlanhla Mahlangu, who composed the music, and was joined on stage by the Soweto Gospel Choir for the amplified version of *Cion:*

Requiem of Ravel's Bolero, a work that brings people together in a time of grief.

In 2021, the Manchester International Festival and Theatre-Rites commissioned me as choreographer for *The Global Playground* with a team of international collaborators. The play invited humanity to celebrate the people they are and the people they cherish, reminding everyone to treat one another with kindness and care.

At the height of Covid-19 in 2021, I co-created *Untold Secrets of the Heart Chamber*, a collaborative film with poet and arts activist Marc Bamuthi Joseph. This 18-minute dance and poetry film ponders on democracy, what grandmothers leave behind, and the safety extended by Black fathers to their sons. At that time I was also a founding chairperson of Sustaining Theatre and Dance Foundation (STAND), a collaborative effort by leaders in the field to mitigate the effects of Covid-19 on artists. We created sustainable projects that allowed artists to earn an income.

The 2021 Edinburgh International Festival commissioned me to produce and direct *Retrace-Retract*, a filmed collaboration with poet Jefferson Tshabalala: retracing South Africa's steps into democracy, the promise of our constitution, and what that document means for ordinary citizens.

2021's *The Valley of Human Sounds*, created for Ballet de Lyon, and 2022's *Black Sun*, created for Ballet Black, both capture the life of communities coming face to face with their ancestors to build a new path of deliverance.

Broken Chord, created with Thuthuka Sibisi in 2022, questions the relationship between the colonised and the coloniser, and our complicity in shaping and shifting the South African narrative. The piece also comments on urgent issues of migration and dispossession.

In 2022, I created *Mandela*, directed by Schele Williams with music by Greg and Shaun Borowsky, produced by the Young Vic in London. This story of the political icon focuses on his family to tell a story of humanity. Also in 2022, I wrote and directed my first musical, *Third World Express* – a political satire of greed and hope.

Most recently, *ZO! MUTE* is a 2023 double-bill created with Vincent Mantsoe:

'We live in a muted state – where those who blow the whistle to uproot corruption find themselves on the firing line.'

Throughout my career, I am proud to count director James Ngcobo among my frequent collaborators. With him, I have created the choreography for award-winning productions such as *The Lion and the Jewel*, *The Hill*, *Crazy for Jazz*, *Thirst*, *Master Harold and the Boys*, *Sunjata* and *Songs of Migration* with Hugh Masekela. I also worked with Ngcobo on the ANC centenary celebration musical, *Tshihumbudzo*, in Bloemfontein.

Full list of works

1994	*Tokolohong*
1995	*Here, Where and There*
1995	*Still Under Their Skin*
1996	*Duplicate*
1996	*Heaven and Earth*
1997	*Dubious*
1998	*Layers of Time*
1999	*Rhythm 1.2.3*
2000	*Rhythm Blues*
2000	*Black Man White Balls*
2000	*Tales of the Mud Wall* with Faustin Linyekula (DRC)
2001	*Southern Comfort*
2002	*Ek sê ... Hola!*
2002	*Strawberry Mouse*
2002	*Miss Thandi*
2003	*Rhythm Colour*
2004	*Ketima*
2005	*Virtually Blond*
2005	*Somehow Delightful*
2006	*Flesh*
2006	*Variations for Vibes, Strings & Pianos* with Akram Khan (United Kingdom)
2006	*Beautiful*

2006	*Beautiful Us*
2007	*Beautiful Me*
2008	*Skeleton Dry Solo*
2009	*Skeleton Dry Group*
2010	*FIFA Pre-Opening Concert (Various)*
2010	*Southern Bound Comfort* with Sidi Larbi Cherkaoui (Belgium)
2012	*Exit/Exist*
2013	*Kudu* with Erik Truffaz
2014	*Fullmoon* with Luyanda Sidiya
2015	*Rain Dance* with Luyanda Sidiya
2015	*Lonely Together* created with Roberto Olivan (Spain)
2016	*Joys of Sharing* with Wouter Kellerman and Simphiwe Dana
2017	*Cion: Requiem of Ravel's Bolero* with Nhanhla Mahlangu
2018	*Rise*
2018	*The Head and The Load* with William Kentridge
2019	*Tree* with Idris Elba and Kwame Kwei-Armah (United Kingdom)
2021	*The Valley of Human Sound*
2021	*Play* with Sue Buckmaster
2022	*Black Sun*
2022	*Broken Chord* with Thuthuka Sibisi
2023	ZO! MUTE

Musicals choreographed

2009 *Crazy for Jazz* with producer Rosie Katz
2010 *Songs of Migration* produced by The Market Theatre
2017 *King Kong* produced by The Fugard Theatre
2022 *Mandela* produced by The Young Vic
2022 *Third World Express* produced by Shadrack Bokaba and Joburg Theatre

Plays choreographed with James Ngcobo

2007 *The Hill*
2008 *The Lion and The Jewel*
2011 *Master Harold and The Boys*
2011 *Sunjata*
2012 *Thirst*
2012 *The Suitcase*
2013 *Nongogo*
2014 *The Colored Museum*

Films choreographed

2022 *The Brave Ones* (Netflix)

Films directed

2021 *Retrace-Retract*
2021 *Untold Secrets of the Heart Chamber* with Marc Bamuthi Joseph

Gregory in early 2000, after winning the Standard Bank Young Artist Award for Dance. These are the books that helped him understand the complexities of South Africa.

Appendix 2
Awards and accolades

2023: Artfluence Human Rights Award from the Centre for Creative Arts at the University of KwaZulu-Natal in recognition of work which advances respect for human dignity, advocates for human rights and celebrates the human spirit.

2022: Feather Award - Simon Nkoli recipient

2022: Black British Award - Outstanding Production for *Black Sun*, created for Ballet Black

2021: New York City Bessie Awards for Dance - Outstanding Production and

Outstanding Music Composition for *Cion: Requiem of Ravel's Bolero*
2020: Naledi Theatre Awards – Best Dance Production for *Cion: Requiem of Ravel's Bolero*
2020: International Dance Day Author
2019: Holland Festival Audience Choice Award for *Cion: Requiem of Ravel's Bolero*
2017: Chevalier de l'Ordre des Arts et des Lettres (Knight of the Arts & Literature) Award for outstanding work in the arts.
2014: New York City Bessie Award for Dance – Outstanding Music Composition in a dance production for *Exit/Exist*
2012: Silver Standard Bank Ovation Award for *MAYHEM*
2012: Tunki Award for Leadership in Dance
2011: Dance Manyano Best Choreographer of the Decade Award
2007: Gauteng MEC Award – Best Choreography in a Contemporary Style for *Beautiful Me*
2007: Gauteng MEC Award – Most Outstanding Presentation of a New Work for *Beautiful Me*

2005: Gauteng MEC Award – Choreographer of the Year for *Beautiful Us*
2004: Finalist – Daimler Chrysler Choreography Competition
2004: Rolex Mentor & Protégé Finalist
2002: FNB Vita Choreographer of The Year for *Southern Comfort* and *Ek sê ... Hola!*
2002: Standard Bank Young Artist Award for Dance; Finalist, Daimler Chrysler Choreography Award; Appointed: Associate Artistic Director at Moving into Dance.
2001: FNB VITA Best Choreography for *Southern Comfort*
2000: FNB VITA Most Outstanding Presentation of an Original Contemporary Work for *Rhythm Blues*
1999: FNB VITA Choreographer of the Year for *Rhythm 1.2.3*
1997: Phillip Stein Young Choreographers Grant
1994: Dance Umbrella Fringe Choreography Award for *Heaven and Earth*
1993: Dance Umbrella Pick of Stepping Stones Choreography Award for *Where, Here and There*

1988: Full Scholarship to study at Performing Arts Research and Training Studios (PARTS) in Belgium from the Flemish Ministry

Cion: Requiem of Ravel's Bolero *theatre production, inspired by Zakes Mda's character Toloki, with Greg's protégé Musa Motha lifted high (photo by John Hogg)*

A note from Lorato Trok

Gregory Maqoma and I are just ten months apart in age, both just children during the Soweto uprisings of 1976, but our upbringing and experiences are worlds apart. Gregory grew up in Soweto, the cradle of both political activism and entertainment in South Africa. I grew up in the 'homelands', the former Bantustan of Bophuthatswana, oblivious – by government design – to the political violence going on in the country.

When South Africa became a democracy in 1994, the Black community had a lot of learning to do, because so much had been prohibited under the previous repressive regime. For the first time, we could read books that had been banned, listen to music we'd not been meant to hear, go to places that had been whites-only enclaves. And we were exposed to new genres of the arts, like contemporary dance. Theatre. Choreography. It hasn't been an easy road, and of course some areas of culture are still prohibitively expensive and too remote for most Black people to access easily. It's worse for rural areas and small-town communities.

I've always loved the arts, entertainment, and reading all kinds of books. I learned about Gregory Maqoma from reading newspapers while I was still a librarian and archivist at the Kuruman Moffat Mission. I followed his career for many years, intrigued by this beautiful, dark-skinned man who was so bold and unapologetic in his career choice: contemporary dance and choreography. Back then, I'd never met a Black man or woman, let alone an African, who was involved in the kind of dance that Gregory was making. He was an anomaly.

I hadn't seen any of Gregory's dance pieces live, but I read every newspaper article about him, watched television shows that featured him or his productions, and listened to his radio interviews. I was in awe! I would never have imagined I would come to write a book about him, or even be in his presence. But how is it possible that an artist like Gregory Maqoma, who has graced the art scene locally and internationally for three decades, does not have a dozen books written about him? Picture books so that little children can see someone who looks like them dancing; books for all the young people he has inspired and will continue to inspire; books to showcase to the world this treasure that South Africa possesses? The country needs many more books on the likes of Gregory Maqoma.

And others: even though he bears the torch as the most successful dancer in South Africa and arguably Africa, there are many astonishing dancers whose stories are crying out to be told. Dance is African, and African stories are plentiful, diverse and celebratory; they don't only involve atrocities, poverty and dictators. I hope this book is the first of many that lift up and celebrate our African cultural heroes.

*The Vuyani Dance Company admin team
From left: Siyandiswa Dakoda (marketing and production),
Lindiwe Letwaba (CEO) and Gregory*

Bibliography

Greg Maqoma, 'Beyond the Euphoria of Movement', TEDxJohannesburg Salon, Theme: Disruptors, https://youtu.be/XubYaoshp6s, 18 August 2016

L. Watterson, R. Sassen & T Greer (eds), *Looking Back to Move Forward: Celebrating 20 Years of an Innovative Contemporary African Dance Company*, Creative Feel/DeskLink Media and Vuyani Dance Theatre, Johannesburg, 2019

Timothy J. Stapleton, 'Reluctant Slaughter: Rethinking Maqoma's Role in the Xhosa Cattle-Killing (1853-1857)', *The International Journal of African Historical Studies* 26, no. 2, 1993

Timothy J. Stapleton, *Xhosa Resistance to Colonial Advance, 1798-1873*, Jonathan Ball, Johannesburg, 1994

Dressed in Maxhosa for the theatre production of Broken Chord, inspired by the first South African choir to tour the UK in 1891 (photo by Moeletsi Mabe)

Photo by Marijke Willemse

About the authors

Gregory Vuyani Maqoma became interested in dance in the late 1980s as a means to escape the growing political tensions in Soweto, South Africa, where he was born. He started his formal dance training in 1990 at Moving into Dance, where he became the Associate Artistic Director in 2002. He founded Vuyani Dance Theatre (VDT) in 1999 while undertaking a scholarship at the Performing Arts Research and Training Studios (PARTS) in Belgium, under the direction of Anne Teresa de Keersmaeker. Maqoma has established himself as an internationally renowned dancer, choreographer, teacher and director.

Greg has received numerous awards, among these the Standard Bank Young

Artist Award for dance in 2002; the Tunkie Award for Leadership in Dance (2012); New York City's premier dance award, the Bessie, for *Exit/Exist* for original music composition (2014); and the Chevalier de L'Ordre des Artes et des Lettres (Knight of the Arts & Literature) Award in 2017 from the French government. Maqoma celebrates his fiftieth birthday in 2023 – this book, together with his children's picture book, *The Joy Dancer*, are two of the legacy projects he has curated to mark the occasion.

Lorato Trok is an expert in early literacy and developing reading-for-pleasure books for young children and teens. She has more than 20 years' experience in publishing, writing, editing, translation and story development in children's and young adults' literature. Lorato is also a creative-writing facilitator and has led multilingual writing workshops in South Africa, Zambia, Lesotho, Swaziland, Kenya and the United States for teachers, students, writers and librarians.

She is also an award-winning translator and editor, and one of her books for teens was a 2021 United Nations Sustainable

Development Goals Book Club (African Chapter) pick. In May 2022, De Gruyter.com, an independent academic digital publisher and research platform, profiled Lorato as one of 28 Women in African Publishing and the Book Trade in their journal, *The African Book Publishing Record*, Volume 48, Issue 2.

Gregory flying at 50 (photo by Arthur Dlamini)